The Relationship Code
for Everything

OrangeBooks Publication

Smriti Nagar, Bhilai, Chhattisgarh - 490020

Website: **www.orangebooks.in**

First Edition, 2020

ISBN: 978-93-90169-13-9

Price: Rs.633.00

Printed in India

THE RELATIONSHIP CODE

FOR EVERYTHING

LEENA CHANDAN

OrangeBooks Publication
www.orangebooks.in

This One's for You – My Lord, Guru, Family & All the Beautiful Angels who make this World a Wonderful & Meaningful place to live in. ☺

In Gratitude to Sai Baba of Shirdi & Jaya Wahi, My Reiki Guru, who nurtured me like her baby with care and compassion when my times were tough.

Hanuman – The Lord of Strength known for His Valiance– Any task gets accomplished with His Blessings. (I promise to share His valour with anyone I talk to, and I chant Hanuman Chalisa eleven times each day to Heal the World.

Special Thanks to Ramchandra Guruji who taught me Yoganidra. This practice, combined with attending life coaching seminars & reading books, helped me discover myself.

> *"We are each of us Angels with only one wing and we can fly only by embracing each other."*
>
> *-Unknown*

Art by Sarah-L-B

About The Author

Leena is an author, coach and storyteller on relationships. She has been associated with the Coaching industry since 2015. She believes life's best learning moments come during the most challenging times. She leverages her life story to share her transformation and best practices to help people find courage to build a new world for themselves and others around them. The power of paying forward what you learn, mutually adding value to each other's lives in a way that you gain momentum in Teamwork is the magic she wants to spread through her work.

About The Book

Where is the journey of your life taking you? Are you steering its ship toward where you'd like to go? What if you could?

In The Relationship Code for Everything, author Leena Chandan shows you how you can take the wheel of your life, and then point your ship straight up to the stars! You'll learn that the secret to living the life of your dreams begins with the most important relationship you'll ever have – the one you have with yourself.

The guidance offered here will stay with you long after you finish reading, with inspiring and effective steps you can take, beginning today, to change how you view and pursue a meaningful and fulfilling life.

First, you will learn how you can deeply nourish your whole being by becoming GIVERS to Self. Then you will discover how to transform every facet of your life while mindfully pointing it in the direction YOU want it to go by following the wisdom outlined in the 22 Golden Nuggets. These will help you build and sustain positive momentum as you reinvent yourself and create new opportunities in your life for happiness and success.

It's often said that life is a journey, not a destination, so let's enjoy the journey! When you make daily effort toward creating your own happiness, your reward will be the joy of a collection of bright moments strung together like pearls, far beyond a mindless, mundane life. This joy will become the precious gift you give to yourself, and get to lovingly receive, as you daily pave and walk the path of your new life.

Table Of Contents

Soulfinder Leena Chandan's debut book, The Relationship Code for life, is your personal guide to investigating and supporting the most important relationship you will ever have – with yourself. Meeting Leena was a magical experience for me from the start, a serendipitous greeting of our two souls as we each stand on the precipice of our new lives. I felt so uplifted reading her words! The tools she provides for self-inquiry and self-actualization are encouraging and practical, and full of such enthusiasm and zest for engaging with life, even with challenges and obstacles that can feel so daunting and leave us overwhelmed. In her pages I found a wise coach, a supportive cheerleader, and a caring friend. And finishing the book isn't the end – she invites her readers to join her online so we might together continue our journeys of self-realization in a cooperative community committed to bolstering one another as we hold each other accountable for the steps we dedicate ourselves to in order to become our best and true selves. I have every confidence that this book will bless your life as it has mine. Leena's genuine character and warm demeanour shines through every word, and her generosity in sharing her knowledge and guidance is a precious gift. I look forward to continuing to manifest our dreams together, and I know you will, too.

With joy,
Erin R Lund
Editor, Sunshine Editorial Services

Introduction

This book is an amazing inspiration to keep within your sight at all times. It is good to keep going from one topic to another and learning more about each topic and creating it deeply within you. This will create a new perspective and give way to a new path. Surely, one thing we all share is that we all want to grow and improve.

My intention is for this book to create such an impact that people remember, follow and forward it to their future generations as a Code to beautifully creating life in a way that they move forward through life; and stop looking back. I love the way PM Narendra Modi describes this time of Conscious Living as taking care of nature as our responsibility, moving forward as Prakruti (in alignment with nature) and not moving backward as Vikruti (against nature). This ensures we walk the right path and set the best example for our future generations.

I went from working in the garment industry to running a business in fashion, to joining the corporate world. When I got jaundice in September 2018 I started to think about everything I deserve to give myself, and what exactly I could become. I quit my job and sketched my path. My search did not last long, as I knew I wanted to do something that would make me happy, enliven my soul, and showcase my creativity. So, I made the decision to take a Leap of Faith and write this book. I am so glad I did! And, this is just one of my new creations. I am also offering Coaching programs with Habits, relationships and more.

I believe it is very important to embrace the perspective that anything you need to accomplish or overcome is possible for you, no matter your past or current circumstance. This begins with accepting complete responsibility for every aspect of your life and refusing to blame anyone else. This helps you develop personal power to create anything in life. It is very important for you to know that no matter what is happening in your life in any given moment, you are meant to be in that exact situation. Remember that it is temporary, and that the experience is for you to learn from so you can become the person you are meant to be.

I would like to take the opportunity to thank my family and friends who took care of me with so much warmth and compassion when times were extremely tough, and I thank myself for walking the path of challenges. I was inspired to do everything to the best of my ability and resolve my life for a great future.

As motivational speaker Tony Robbins says,

"To make profound changes in your life, you need inspiration or desperation."

I hope you enjoy reading my book and it is an inspiration for your life. ☺

The Relationship Code for Everything

- Soulfinder Leena Chandan
(Love, Matter, Celebrate)

A Path toward Skyrocketing Your Way to an Extraordinary Life

> *"The greatest discovery of my generation is that a human being can alter his life by altering his attitude."*
>
> *– William James.*

I have learned that altering your attitude is not only about doing the same things in a different manner, it is about encouraging oneself to expand to new horizons and a new point of view while taking charge of your life to add more value to yourself and others around you. While it is true that grit, will power, practice and talent are required to take you to your next level; identifying your strengths and weaknesses as a foundation to begin this journey is necessary. And yet, not many of them achieve success as the focus is only on ME. True transformation also demands adding value, leading others, managing competing priorities - it is service and meaningful contribution to others.

How can you add value? Some considerations might be: BECOME AN ABOVE-AVERAGE PERSON, DEVELOP AN ABOVE-AVERAGE HANDSHAKE, DEVELOP AN ABOVE-AVERAGE SMILE, DEVELOP AN ABOVE-AVERAGE ENTHUSIASM, DEVELOP AN ABOVE-AVERAGE INTEREST IN OTHER PEOPLE, DEVELOP AN ABOVE-AVERAGE INTENSITY TO WIN. These will change everything.

At this point, we actually start attracting new things in life.

Preface

Why "The Relationship Code for Everything in Life"

The simple reason is this:

When you start living in the present, your success with everything depends on your relationship with every small thing that is around you, and all that you have taken for granted. Start respecting yourself, even your supposedly unlikeable enemy or competition and see the good in them. When you do so, you will see a shift in the vibration around you that will change your life. Once you start practising the habit of being "givers to self" as explained in this book later, you will start becoming aware of your relationship with everything around you.

I have been blessed to learn how to overcome all my fears and limiting beliefs. I want to make it easier for people to understand what's stopping them when they cannot move ahead, and what they can do about it. There are many people who are tremendously uncertain about how to get ahead in life, and which decisions are right for them, their families and their careers. People want to scale up, and at the same time they are wiped out. They are driven, and yet don't exactly know what they want. They desire to go for their dreams, yet they are afraid they'll be judged for their ideas, or will fail if they try.

For others, many are living happy, wonderful lives, but consistency is a problem. While they may feel capable and confident, there is always a steep cliff on the other side. They are wondering how to reach heightened and sustained growth and success. They desire guidance in improving their wellbeing and in holistically advancing their lives and careers.

Sometimes you take on many projects, yet end up binge watching three seasons on Netflix instead. Sometimes you wonder how other people are succeeding while going from one project to the next, no matter what obstacles are thrown their way. It seems like despite whatever context, company or industry they find themselves in, they'll win. What's their secret? Their secret is Habits, and their RELATIONSHIP with EVERYTHING AND EVERYONE AROUND THEM.

The times today feel incredibly chaotic as expectations, ground rules and everything are in constant flux. Your boss, your lover, your customer, everyone wants something new now. It is not as simple as it used to be, and if it is, odds are a computer or a robot will replace you soon. Also, everything is connected, so messing up one thing messes up an entire network, which is public and global, in a world where certainties are down and expectations are up.

Leap Of Faith

How are you planning to get more out of your life?

I heard this at an event in 2016, and since then I have this on my white board in my room. I read it every day:

Simple step of REFORMED BELIEF >>> MASSIVE POTENTIAL >>> MASSIVE ACTION >>> MASSIVE RESULTS.

I used to be someone who did not want much for myself. I was also a complete introvert. I worked night shifts for eight years just to pay my bills, without feeling any need to explore my true potential. I thank the wonderful organizations where I spent a huge part of my youth for giving me the opportunity to contribute, for believing in me and for including me in their journey.

Just as many others have and do in that state, I self-sabotaged my career and relationships by starting out in unfulfilling places early on in life. My biggest realisation was that I never gave myself time to work on myself and the relationships with other people, with excuses of not wanting to socialise much or being an introvert. I was not open to sharing. I would worry how someone would judge me. Of course, I resolved a lot of this in the corporate world when I mingled with many people as we discussed and exchanged thoughts with each other. And in my journey of coaching I noticed my clients experiencing these limitations too. It is not wrong to have limitations. It is important to become aware of any limitation, as this is how one's journey begins. So go all out in your search for the right Coach -- share your views, learn about different elements of the industry, ask them how they managed to land a deal, etc.

Sometimes when you experience a failure in life, you start telling yourself that you are a failure. Such a series of failures can break you down, but only until you realise and understand that life is all about failing and succeeding. Instead of getting bogged down by the failures, get up and find something new to do each time you fail, and success is sure to come. And with every win or success you get, go ahead and celebrate! Once you understand this, you will become unstoppable, and nothing can stop you from creating and achieving multiple possibilities. One tough lesson for me was learning that while it is good to run, I didn't want to run so fast that I missed out the most important things in life– my RELATIONSHIPS WITH EVERYTHING AND EVERYONE – and the value I can create for every small thing around me.

Deep down in my heart I prayed that I live a life of COMPLETE SELF EXPRESSION EVERY SINGLE DAY ON THIS PLANET. By writing this book and helping people in this process I surely know my journey has begun. ☺

I felt stuck in so many ways that I could not understand what was happening to me.

I asked myself crazy questions like whether I can succeed in life. I counted myself out as a victim.

Thanks to all the Coaching programs I attended, I pushed myself out of my comfort zone in every way I could. I ran here and there. Do you know why? As my soul was not in peace, I was not clear about what I wanted, the love of my life crossed me, i didn't notice and thankfully these clearances helped us get back and my family also hasn't seen me for many years. I ran and ran and ran in the beginning from one program to another. With much gratitude, I am happy to spend quality time with my family now.

Life Coach Arfeen Khan wrote, "BARRIERS EXIST ONLY IN THE MIND, AND THE POWER TO TRANSCEND THEM ALSO LIES IN THE MIND."

It's truly in our hands to keep creating the opposite of every negative thought we repeatedly think in order to trick our minds into being positive.

We overcome limiting beliefs by using multiple strategies. First, identify the limiting beliefs that are stopping you from getting what you want or are obstacles to your goals. Then develop unshakeable self- confidence that you will be able to achieve your stated goal. To strengthen this, please know that it needs your complete focus because whatever you focus on expands. If you constantly keep telling yourself that you're bold and assertive, you will become so, and nothing will stop you.

So please, open your mind, develop a clear plan of action and break it down into potential steps. Finally, ensure that you work towards that goal by doing these things consistently.

Some limiting beliefs are:

- I can't.
- I'll never be rich.
- I'll always have to work a job.
- I need to be a particular way to be loved.

Also, it is said that we choose our happiness. I would say Happiness is not only a choice, it is a RESPONSIBILITY. Do anything it takes for you to attain your happiness. Search for the right Coach who can guide you if you feel incomplete, keep yourself accountable to someone who you trust, and make sure you achieve it without fail. Be part of a community that can help you develop as an individual. Write freely to people, share your problems, discuss with someone, get comfortable with being yourself, or take up a hobby that can help you to better be in the moment.

Also be aware, this means living in the present moment. In his book, "Solve for Happy," engineer and author Mo Gawdat calls it a "cat's view of time." Keeping this in mind makes it easier to keep coming back to the now. It simply means, if it is 1 pm, time for lunch. If it is 8 pm, time for dinner. This is how animals live with time. The simplest way to apply this is to create a schedule and follow it – do what needs to be done at each time. Most people get sad when they live in the past or future.

Notes:

Your past is really nothing but a record of moments we call memories. It is an unreliable collection.

So be conscious and find ways to resolve it to work on living in the moment. Going into the future, it is good to have a schedule, a plan just like the ship needing a navigator to reach a specific place. It is also important to be obsessed with getting what you want in a way that creates your reality; however, also understand that you are not currently living there. Happy emotions are mostly anchored by being in the present.

Close your eyes, Imagine the present is a huge golden ball of light, and a very expensive and valuable diamond which you won't get back even if you pay millions for it. Do you see the past or future in it? No, what you have here is the PRESENT and whatever can you create for yourself in that golden ball. What needs to be done at THIS moment? How can you ensure you can do it with a smile on your face? Constantly creating such things in your mind can help you be in the present. How can you add value to what you're doing?

Ask yourself some questions:

Where to; now?

Why are others climbing faster than I am? Does it always have to feel like such a grind? Am I truly living my best life? What does living an extraordinary life mean to me?

People told me to work hard, be passionate, focus on strengths, be grateful. Doing all of this shows you're taking action that is needed, but you only can work hard up to a point. Isn't it true that there are billions of hard workers at the bottom of the pile? There are people who have strengths and passion and still struggle? Do you think they need to be more grateful or mindful? Or is it their attitude? Every individual's story about how they do things is different. You need to get deep into yourself to know why you behave the way you do.

I am so happy for these programs. I got back to living a normal life with a good personal-work life balance and I got the opportunity to learn everything I wanted to get a career I want with clients who trust their path, are willing to make a difference in their own lives, and are gaining the ability and confidence to achieve anything and everything they want. I read self-help books, listened to a lot of podcasts related to motivation, and attended several seminars and got coached from some of the best in the industry.

What helps you become world class to create a lasting impact beyond yourself?

How can you generate the confidence you need to reach the next level of success?

How can you be happy and sustain success over the long term?

My answer is, Habits, because they are foundational to creating both an alignment and commitment to certain chosen practices. I have picked the most simple and best habits that can tune you in to a higher vibe.

As a Life Coach, it is very important for me to serve the mindset in a way that the client is really able to get what they want from life. Also, I don't know whether it's a boon or a curse to be unable to pay the bills for a few months while switching from a job to following your dreams, but certainly to do what I am doing gives me undying confidence to share that I got here with a lot of courage. This waiting period towards success is super amazing and is showering me with unlimited knowledge to find my path that I'd waited forever to find. I love every bit of it. Apparently, sitting at home, I am learning several times more than I ever have, and running a business today makes me an independent person. I really did this based on two things that author and speaker Steve Harvey says:

1) "Ask and You shall Receive" (from the Bible)

What we do is ask once and lose faith if we don't get it. The magic begins when you constantly in good faith keep asking until you get it. Let me tell you it was not an easy journey, I have been asking Nature for thirteen years now – but it is POSSIBLE, and by asking constantly, I achieved a lot.

It is important to remember that we have nothing to lose, we only gain by asking. I remember a time when I was not promoted in spite of being a top performer amongst my peers. I approached the VP and we had a conversation. I shared with him the consistency levels I maintained and the accolades I won, and then, I got my promotion. This is clear indication that if you're not satisfied with something, get over all the hesitation and ask for what you want. Also, you will be glad to know that what you want is what wants you too. Nature wants to provide you with it and it is already available for you. It is for you to make it come into your life for real.

Similarly, I met a client at a cafe and there was no space at all. I insisted the waitress just seat us at a table if they could, as we did not have many options to travel to another place then. She had refused him initially when he had requested this, but when I insisted, she did it. My client was amazed that I could get it done. I was assertive about what I wanted.

Sometimes, we may have to ask for money from our families if we are starting a business. This is the most difficult state to be in, to have to depend on them to take care of our expenses. It is very difficult to believe anything good can happen but yes, you have to have courage and tell yourself it is possible, and that you want this temporary constraint to shape your life for better. It is important to remember that this state has come for a reason: to learn, earn and move on.

2) When you jump out of an airplane, the parachute doesn't open immediately, you have to trust, and float in air for a few seconds while you wait for it to open up. Imagine your whole life is 70 years, and if you contribute those few years of struggle, it is equivalent to those seconds in your life's timeline. However, you need to have faith and trust that on the other side, a lot of beautiful things are waiting to fill you with bliss, happiness and abundance.

So, here's the wait for my beautiful parachute to open up in a way that brings unlimited joy and pride in my parent's eyes for having me as their child. ☺ I have tears in my eyes when I say this because I never thought myself to be a good child – I thought I was a failure who could never get anything in life, without seeing that Nature or Universe has actually gifted me with everything, even more than what I could have asked for.

Apparently, my journey of knowing and searching for myself began when my friend asked me.......

Do you think you're incapable of achieving anything?

Do you think you're small and you can't do anything?

Do you really think you're not beautiful?

Little did he know my answers would be yes, I did think I was incapable, I did think I was small and couldn't do anything, and I also thought I was not beautiful, WHILE THE WHOLE WORLD AROUND ME THOUGHT I WAS BEAUTIFUL, and there were people who even wanted to BE me. SAD STORY. It is all in the mind and how we grew up that determine the thoughts and beliefs we carry that made us into who we have become.

I am sure there are lot of people who don't know how to get ahead and can't make decisions for themselves. They're working so hard, but they are just not breaking the ice. They are driven, but don't know exactly what they want. They have a desire to go for their dreams, yet they are afraid of being judged a failure. However, the GOOD NEWS IS THROUGH THE PROCESS OF GETTING

COACHED, YOU CAN RESOLVE YOUR LIFE FOR A BIGGER VISION. I am on a mission to reach 500,000 people who will know themselves better through this book.

Also, I want to create a small example related to breaking the ice that I spoke of above. It is a fact that 70% of our body is made of water. Now, imagine yourself standing on ice that you're not able to break. Does that ever happen? No, it can't because ice starts melting and pouring water on it makes it melt faster. Similarly, whether we like it or not, life will keep flowing and reach its end. Are you able to relate this to your life? Are you willing to melt that ice which has formed in your brain due to cultural norms, family views, society, friends, or beyond everything by yourself?

Furthermore, today when I stand strong with nothing in my hand I see I have everything, and I see my path very clearly. But yes, just like everyone has a journey, I had my own difficulties to overcome. When you are gunning for something new, make sure you have resolved your past in every way you can to make a clear future. Keep visualising that you have a broom and a sweeping kit to clean your brain. Every time you clean something in your home, visualise yourself cleaning unwanted things from your brain too. This practice slowly makes everything that is unwanted vanish, and you speed up your way to achieving more, giving way to ncw things in life.

Talk to yourself on a regular basis to create a more enlightened pathway of thought. This has a huge impact on the on our quality of life. It will make you aware of the personal dialogue you have going on within you every minute of the day, and allow you to promise yourself to make it better every time.

I would love to share with you the choicest life lessons I have learned which have given me the courage to tell everyone that they can stand strong. I hope you enjoy every bit of reading this book.

Notes:

Self-Love

> **"Self-love is not selfish; you cannot truly love another until you know how to love yourself."**

As a success-obsessed society we have grown to believe that being average -- being like most other people – is not good enough. Just know that we don't need to be supermodels or champions all the time. Even supermodels at times don't feel good enough because there's someone more attractive than that. Being average feels frightening because those who are above average can deprive us of the opportunity to succeed in this competitive world. Yet it is not at all true that someone needs to be average and someone above. Pushing oneself unrealistically is a sure way to suffering, which will compound stress. Take a break and ask yourself if you would treat someone you love this way. No, right? You would give them warmth and reassurance. Then why do you treat yourself so badly? Assume you're a mother, and a mother would treat her babies with intensive care and compassion, would keep them safe, and her soft touch and gentle communication would create feel-good hormones that will allow her babies to perform better. Treat yourself like a loved child ☺ and accept yourself, appreciate yourself, and then keep trying again and again and take new actions regardless of the outcome.

I know this to be true because there was a time when I could not connect well with people and I had not realised that I hadn't given enough to myself, and hence my relationship with everyone around me looked disturbed.

The only best way to develop self-love is to embrace all the good, bad, and ugly you go through, and hug yourself in front of the mirror every single morning and smile as every event has made you the way you are. (Consider even the painful experiences to be Blessings in Disguise.)

Also know you are here on this planet to make a difference. Add as much value as you can to this world around that is in turmoil. If we can collectively become conscious citizens living to our fullest potential, you'll change your world and the world around you. We'll surely reduce the burden this planet is carrying. Many (as I used to be) are comfortable with mediocrity. They avoid living a greater life, one that's beyond the norm. A greater life requires you to become the best version of yourself by breaking the imaginary boundaries that hold you, touching the realms of Unthinkable Infinite Possibilities. Strive to become better than who you were yesterday.

Impress yourself, not other people.

Stretch yourself to new horizons.

Test yourself in different waters.

Gauge where you stand from 1 to 5 in Family & Friends, Relationship (partner), Personal Development, Health, Career, Wealth, Fun and Spirituality. Then, see what you can do to raise the bars in the lowest ratings to strike a balance.

Every single day, be a better person than yesterday – in competition with yourself, not with the expectations the world has of you. Wake up every single day with this desire and fire in your mind, and stay committed.

Remember, true greatness is not in material possessions, it is that which brings purpose, love, appreciation and happiness. Create a positive impact in the world. The material world will follow.

There is a saying in Sanskrit: "Aham Brahmasmi"

It means, I am The Absolute. I am The Creator of My Life. There is no duality, we are one with God and in that God is everything, and every other human being too is a part of that Huge Creation – so we have to live as one organism.

It also means that since Life is without any inherent meaning, meaning can be mindfully given. For example, say your grandfather's gramophone sits on a table in your house. It's been there for years and your mom treasures it very much. However, you may not be that attached to it as you don't have any memories with it yourself. However, your mom, she'll tell you about her meaning for it, how her dad used it every night before sleeping and how much he loved it, how it's the most beautiful treasure she has, etc. Consider all this to be meaning that she herself gave to that gramophone, but you as the third generation are not attached to it.

You may want to sell it off at an antique store or for scrap. The simple reason is you haven't connected with it, so you have not given any meaning to it. The best way to deal with every situation you face is to start asking, what meaning does this hold for me? And then once you recognise that meaning deep down, you can keep it, or discard it and give it a new meaning that you would like better.

This could be used for every area of your life, especially relationships. For example, if you and your spouse are fighting about something, you could just stop talking altogether, or say what you want to say in a funny way to flip the situation with humour. It is in your hands to make it a humorous conversation or a red hot boiling one. ☺

The best mindset for dealing powerfully with such situations starts with self-love.

I LOVE MYSELF SO
MUCH THAT MY LOVE
CREATES RIPPLES OF
PURE LOVE FOR
EVERYONE IN THE
WORLD AROUND ME
- LEENA CHANDAN

Self-love means you're able to strike a balance between work and play, action and patience, spending and saving, laughter and seriousness. A failure to achieve this balance leaves you exhausted, frustrated.

Imagine a world where every individual loves themselves so much that they are not threatened by other people's opinions, or any differences like race, education, lack of possessions, religious beliefs, etc. It is for us to wake up to a world of love beyond shame, guilt, or self-doubt so that we can create a fearless world with lots of happiness.

There are two elements to self-love. The first is that you accept yourself as you are with compassion, and the second is that you focus on taking the needed action to become how you want to be. Self-love also demands that you think about loving others unconditionally. For example, a family member may have annoying habits at times; this would never mean that you love them any less. Accept them as they are and learn from their flaws. If a particular habit is affecting them, avoid being harsh; instead, support them to bring positive changes. I was so glad that my family supported, loved and accepted me for the rebel that I had become and it is surely due to their blessings that I am here today. ☺

True self love can be present in anything from your diet to your spirituality to the way you interact within personal relationships. An understanding of self-love allows you find a balance between mindset and action. Love yourself and life will begin to love you. This will enable you to vibrate higher. Once you vibrate higher you can use the

Law of Attraction (The Secret to getting what you want). The other condition to the Law is being positive about the result while in the process of believing the law. This is the phase where you end up being two different people experiencing extreme highs and lows. Sometimes it feels so messy that you 'll question if the law actually works. Sometimes it's so messy that you'll find yourself shouting at people in your family, throwing things, or resisting anything that comes your way. You'll surely want to leave everything behind. The only option is to wait and let that phase pass by – engage yourself in becoming the best version of yourself at this point, and if you did not get something it was genuinely not meant to be, or the reason you needed or wanted it was not right. However, you'll get the best of what is meant for sure and you'll surely end up in a space of being a Shining Light. ☺

In the process, be conscious of the Law of Vibration. The Universe responds to your vibration. It will return whatever energy you put out. The Universe is clearly an ocean of vibrations. If it is so, our thoughts, actions, feelings are all a vibration and we can control our reality. We really need to believe in something as if it were true and increase chances of its becoming our living reality. Our thoughts, emotions, words and actions should be aligned to what we want. For example, to listen to a particular radio channel, you have to tune into that same number, or else you'll end up listening to a different station. The best way to identify what frequency you're on is through your emotions. Emotions show a true reflection of your energy, and finding a pathway toward understanding your emotions better is about having a consistent practice of Habits.

Habits to Help Tune into Positivity and Overcome Negative Emotions:

- Laughing
- Physical touch with a loved one
- Listening to uplifting music
- Spreading kindness
- Sleeping deeply
- Surrounding yourself with positive people
- Body language – trick your brain into smiling when you feel like you can't
- Give yourself some alone time to reset
- Stay away from gossip and drama
- Stay hydrated
- Observe your emotions frequently
- Be present in the moment

Question – Which habits get you quick wins, and what are the long-term practices that make you stand out?

> *"If I had six hours to chop down a Tree, I would spend the first four hours sharpening the Axe."*
>
> *- Abraham Lincoln.*

MY manager shared this quote with me and it deeply moved something in me.

This sharpening the Axe is a strength Multiplier. I truly started working endlessly in every possible way to sharpen the axe with all the knowledge I could attain. I have also outlined some steps in the form of a concept "GIVERS TO SELF" for you to practice.

Notes:

Part I
Being "GIVERS" To Self

> *"Nothing has any power over me other than that which I give it through my conscious thoughts."*
>
> *- Tony Robbins*

My friend shared this with me once that as human beings we have an average of 60,000 thoughts in a single day, and guess what - Not all those thoughts are ours. The day I heard this, I did a deep study on it, and just like there are lot of frequencies of networks when there are hundreds of cell phones around, similarly there are several neural networks around too at all times – different energies and vibrations. That doesn't mean we start judging the people around us. The only control we have is to keep a check on what we are thinking. The best method is to differentiate every thought you get in a way that you're able to distinguish between what is meant to be practised and what is not meant to be practised or carried. Just keep in mind that what goes around, comes around. So make a decision based on love, so you'll get back love.

This is the simplest way to understand your thought process.

One simple practice you can do is, start writing down any constant thoughts you are having and note if they are negative or positive.

Being a "Giver to Self" comes first, which means practising the following Habits regularly. This consistency is the reason why someone else may be ahead of you, or you are grappling to find a way.

Why Habits? This is the way to improve self-discipline, have accountability, and a keep a record of everything you want to achieve.

How can you become a master of your habits? One of the biggest obstacles for people is that they don't have a strategy for bringing positive habits into their routine, and hence they are not able to master implementing and sustaining positive habits. In return, they don't know what to expect and are not prepared enough to overcome mental and emotional challenges that are part of the process of implementing a new habit. It is that initial pain of consistency, and if they lose or break the habit for a day, they don't want to continue. This is exactly the challenge you need to overcome in order to get to a point of understanding the power of habits. It is a very uncomfortable phase to come through in the beginning and once you win it, there are high possibilities for you to achieve all that you ask for. It takes 21 days to cultivate a habit and 40 days to make it a long-term habit. It is important to make it a continuous long-term part of your routine.

> *"Motivation is what gets you started. Habit is what keeps you going."*
>
> *- Jim Rohn*

The Habits of being **GIVERS TO SELF** has shown that they work with a broad range of personalities, in a lot of situations to create amazing results. It's sure to feel a new sense of vital energy and confidence from knowing where to focus on and how to serve most effectively and specially it would be really magical if you could practice being a "Giver to self" every morning at a specific time.

G - Gratitude, 3 minutes

I - Incantations, 5 minutes

V- Visualisation, 10 minutes

E - Exercise, 10 minutes

R - Reading, 20 minutes

S - Scribing, 5 minutes

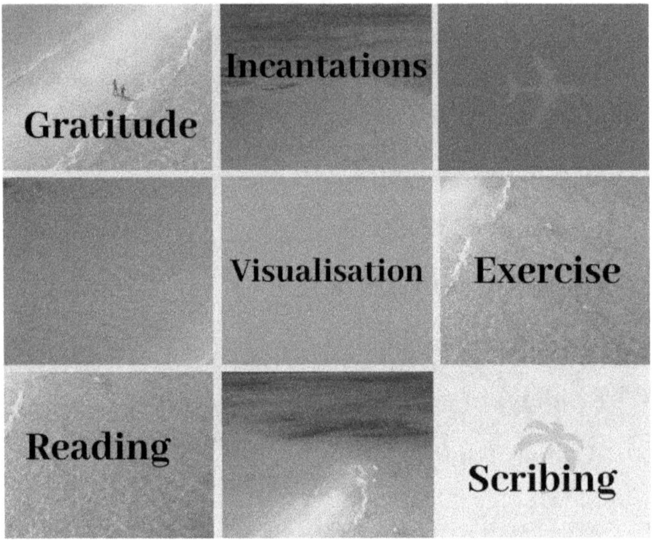

Gratitude
Incantations
Visualisation
Exercise
Reading
Scribing

These practices can fill you up with the best vibrations.

I am sure many of you will have excuses (just like I did) for not doing these, and it's the most difficult thing to build a new habit. It's that dire urge or need for you to overcome the obstacle and get what you want in your life that actually makes you do what it takes. That fire, that passion in you to achieve something in life, having a reason for you to wake up every single day with excitement. Everything will work together. It's necessary for you not to resist giving in to the excuses and take action, as the results will be fulfilling.

Gratitude

> *"Gratitude is the fairest blossom which springs from the soul."*
>
> *– Henry Ward Beecher.*

In simple terms, thankfulness is the ability to show appreciation. It is a state of mind which keeps you happier and feeling more alive. It's about consistently counting blessings every day. Being thankful will become a habit. It's very easy to slip off the hook of gratitude and get into what I call "The Complaining Zone." However, one really needs to put in a lot of effort initially to get into this zone of gratitude, which is surely the beginning of achieving Greatness in any field. It is a vital component of joy and happiness. We create a state of high vibration so we can become magnetic to good things in this state. The practice of meditation (Yoganidra) was the initial gateway for me to enter this zone of Gratitude. This zone also helps us overcome a tag of good or bad and it teaches us to be grateful for all those moments that make up a life. This practice is like a sunshine that breaks through the window into your room and illuminates it when you open the curtains in the morning. It is a vital catalyst that brings about wonders in people's lives. The practice of writing minimum of three things each day that you are thankful for and reading them all when you're feeling low or exhausted gets you back into the Gratitude zone. You can increase the number of things you want to write about that you are grateful for as this becomes a habit. Also, have you heard the saying, "live everyday like it's your last day"? If today was genuinely your last day what would you be telling people? Become that Connoisseur of Gratitude. You might even sometimes create Certificates of Thankfulness for your loved ones.

Some benefits of practicing Gratitude are:

- Helps you to be positively driven
- Allows you to keep a check on the ego
- Let's you enjoy life to the fullest
- Let's you find meaning in life
- Makes you more sociable
- Improves the quality of sleep
- Makes you emotionally stronger
- Enhances and embellishes personality
- Elevates your personal and professional life

Why Gratitude? It's a proven technique that boosts happiness and generates a climate of happiness both inward and outside, fosters physical and psychological health. Brain scans of people who use the expression of Gratitude show lasting changes in the prefrontal cortex.

Practices to follow the path of Gratitude:

- Write a Gratitude journal
- Write 'Thank You' notes to people
- No comparison or competition with others – I compare my abilities with what I was yesterday, and I am in competition with myself
- Own up your flaws – it is okay to be human

- Get adequate rest

- Practise to be on time but don't be obsessed with the clock, the clock was not created to control the man

- Cultivate the habit of recognising the value of every human being

- Remember, life is not a never-ending race

- Most important, value what you have, as not taking it for granted is a responsibility

- Think about people who have inspired you and what about them was most significant

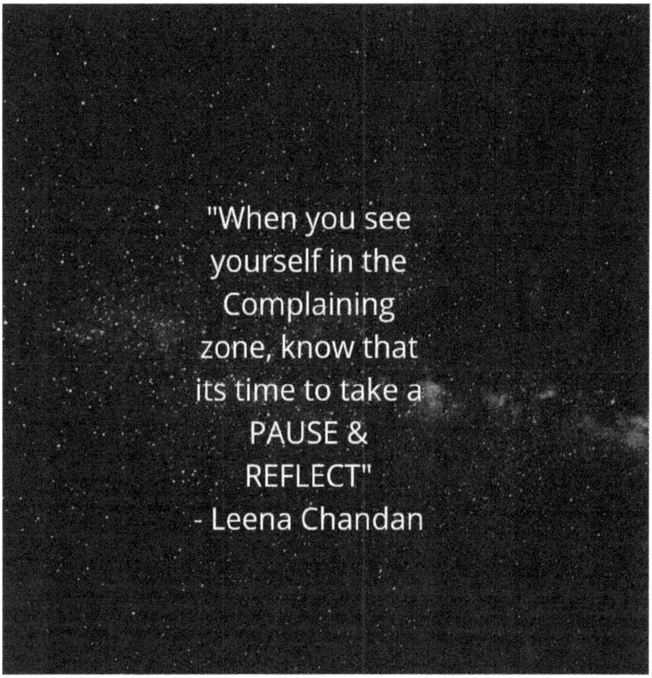

"When you see
yourself in the
Complaining
zone, know that
its time to take a
PAUSE &
REFLECT"
- Leena Chandan

Incantations

> *"Negative things you tell yourself are incantations – turn them into Positive Incantations."*
>
> *– Tony Robbins*

Reaffirming Positive Incantations by simply saying them over and over creates a deep belief in the subconscious mind. It's a conscious process like feeding a program into a computer. These are to be read repeatedly and regularly without fail at all high and low times. Repeating them during good times adds to that vibe and makes it more powerful. It then clears the path by removing weeds from the mind to make the soil fertile so we are able to get more from life. This helps us overcome all those times when we told ourselves that we were not good enough, or considered ourselves incapable of something. Just know for a fact that your body loves you. As a child, we loved every bit of ourselves the way we were. Over time we began listening to what others told us and we got carried away. Practicing this consistently will help overcome all the incapacities that have been created in the mind.

I didn't even know what it meant when I started reading them every day. I just knew that I had to overcome the stage I was in and raise my standard to attract better things. Doing this is a magical technique. Just trust the process, stand in front of the mirror with a smile, and read them over and over. Doing this twice a day is great, however, definitely do so at least once a day.

Some beautiful, life-changing gifts of incantations that you can read regularly are listed below. These are surely my luck charms, and I am opening the doors for you, too, to accept them with Grace and allow them to contribute every single day to making all your days as blissful as they can be.

- I respect everyone and everyone respects me.
- I am a love magnet; I am a money magnet.
- I am very organised in everything I do.
- I have the most amazing, understanding and caring partner who loves me, and, likewise.
- I am whole and complete.
- I am jovial, fun loving and a person of good humour.
- I have a luxurious lifestyle and I easily provide for myself.
- I am very clear with what I am doing and completely satisfied with the career I have.
- I work smart not hard.
- I am an easy-going person with lots of self-love. I manage everything with ease and calm.
- I am a results-oriented person in everything I do.
- I am in a zone of Gratitude and do not complain about my work or other people.
- I am powerful and limitless.
- I am in control of my mind, thoughts and life.
- I am increasingly magnetic to good thoughts, health, wealth, abundance, and prosperity.

- The Universe is filled with Abundance.

- When Nature strengthens Me, everything works for me.

- I resolve relationship issues instead of withdrawing from people over differences.

- I accept, appreciate and love myself. It helps me add value to all my other relationships.

- Today is a great day. It is auspicious. I am celebrating my life.

Checklist for you to complete:

- The most positive people in my life with whom I should spend more time are ...

- High performers in my network are ...

- New routines or hangouts I can create to find more positive and supportive people in my life are....

Visualisation

> *"When you visualize, then you materialize."*
>
> *— Denis Waitley*

A constant commitment to Visualisation or Meditation is a must. It feels like a task initially however, practising it regularly makes your mind calm and less angry, increases your concentration, and develops your awareness of the present moment. The frequency in the brain (driven by the brain's molecular structure) aligns in a particular pattern which make it efficient and helps us get best results.

My journey of Visualisation/meditation started with practising Yoganidra which is a type of sleep meditation. However, I completely understand that people who work are too tired to sit up another 20 minutes to meditate. So, here's the good news: you can play this guided meditation just before you sleep, and do it lying on your back facing the ceiling, with your hands and legs a little apart (the position of Shavaasan in Yoga). The state that Yoganidra puts the mind into is the best altered state to be in. It stores the vibe and programs in your subconscious mind to get ready for the new. The practice of Yoganidra can help create anything, from higher levels of success or health to whatever else you want to visualise and make real.

I have posted a simple guided meditation on anchor podcast > Soulfinder > Please do NOT listen to it while driving. Only listen to it while lying down, as chances are, you may fall asleep listening to it.

Yoganidra is best done when you're just about to sleep or just after you wake up, for, when the mind is in-between the sleep and waking states, it's in an altered state which allows messages to best reach the subconscious mind. This then helps generate actions and words that help you reach your goal. The word Yoga means, "connection or union," and Nidra means, "sleep." We can do any task to our fullest potential when our mind, body and soul are aligned and working together in synchronicity with cosmic energy. This is one of the best meditations for helping attain this alignment. You can also visualise who you need to be, what you need to be, and your current and future goals.

This brings a deeper balance within us which creates perfect equilibrium, developing inner calm and patience.

Also, it is ideal to visualise your answers to these questions, Who are you? What are your needs? What kind of goals you should develop? Visualise them as dreams that have come true for which you have waited forever.

Practicing Visualisation:

- Promotes self-healing. Improves relationships
- Removes negative blocks and toxins from the body.
- Enhances personal power leading to greater awareness.

Once you start practising this regularly, you also won't feel like smoking or drinking much.

45

ITS LIFE
CHANGING AND
WORTH IT TO
WORK ON YOUR
DREAMS
- Soulfinder
Leena Chandan

Notes:

Exercise

> **"The reason I exercise is for the quality of life I enjoy."**
>
> **– Kenneth H Cooper. (Not only to lose fat)**

Every morning exercise increases your blood circulation, gets your heart rate up and fill your lungs with oxygen. Just 15 minutes' brisk walk in front of your mirror standing in one place and a few Jumping Jacks (for those who can) is more than enough, with a few stretches, planks if you can, and/or Suryanamaskar (stretches called Sun Salutation, you can find on Youtube). It also enhances creativity, improves mental clarity and sustains high levels of energy. Stay hydrated and maintain your sleep time. It's good to be healthy and not overdo it. I know people who spend hours together in the gym and build muscles just to get over stress which is over-work.

You may have at some time felt a kind of pain in the centre of your chest, or some uneasiness. Exercising with a walk or run is the best way to keep away from that pain body. Jumping Jacks also help.

Most high performers are more likely to at least exercise three times a week. We all want good health, however, we think we have to trade it for success. That's not true, doing simple things can make you feel energised – mentally, physically, and emotionally.

Reading

> *"I do believe something magical can happen when you read a good book."*
>
> *– JK Rowling*

Read more about other people's reflections and a form of faith in a "higher being" as an emotional survival tactic. Doing so:

- Helps you discover yourself
- Imparts valuable lessons from years of experience
- Improves focus, concentration, and emotional health
- Enhances memory
- Is great source of motivation
- Broadens knowledge, imagination and creativity
- Makes you empathetic and humble
- Gives joy and makes you happy

The most important thing about reading is you learn from experts who have already done what you want to do.

I had a client who used to hate reading books and he complained that it made him doze off. Ideally, books are surely a beginning step for your pathway and opening your mind to new ideas, patterns of thinking. Also, when we are not reading we have a closed mind that is always fighting to keep everything at arm's length. We can learn a lot when we are exposed to other points of view which are different from our own. We become open minded, relaxed and logical.

Many people tell that they can't read because they doze off. If you can't sit in place and read, walk and read, or run and read. Do anything it takes to read a few books.

Scribing

> **Writing in a journal each day allows you to direct your focus to what you accomplished, what you're grateful for and what your committed to doing better tomorrow. This helps you enjoy your journey more deeply each day."**
>
> **– Hal Elrod**

Daily Jounal Writing:

- Gives Clarity
- Improves focus
- Helps you move towards your mission with a lot of energy and high vibe
- Tracks your progress

Questions to consider:

What do you habitually tell yourself when you experience self-doubt or disappointment or feel that you're failing?

What personal and professional routines help you stay focussed, energised, creative, productive and effective?

When you're feeling the pressure of a near-term deadline, how do you maintain or protect your well-being?

Goals are as essential to success as air is to life. No one can achieve success without a goal. No one ever lives without air. It's just as important to get a clear fix on where you want to go. A progressive company plans 15 years ahead. So start your journey and plan your life. It's very important to surrender to that goal and get obsessed with it. It starts auto-generating all that you need over a period of time. It's not easy, there is discomfort- it's there to ensure success.

ITS LIFE
CHANGING AND
WORTH IT TO
WORK ON YOUR
DREAMS
- Soulfinder
Leena Chandan

Notes:

54

Part II

22 GOLDEN NUGGETS COMING YOUR WAY

1. The Three I's: Integrity, Intention And Imagination

INTEGRITY

> *"Integrity is choosing your thoughts and actions based on your values rather than personal gain."*
>
> *- Chris Karcher*

The simplest example could be sitting on the dining table and not eating with integrity. Being present where you are, not phubbing (the practice of ignoring one's companion/ companions in order to pay attention to one's phone or other mobile device) are simple ways of showing integrity, parents apologizing to kids because they were yelled at.

Of course, there are bigger ways to show integrity like being conscious of every small act of harming, etc. and living a conscious lifestyle like not littering on the streets, being mindful of others' needs. It's also about being conscious in every act of business and personal life.

The two most common words associated with a person of integrity are honesty and trustworthiness.

It can also be explained as wholeness, harmony and completeness to one's identity. A person with integrity would live completely in alignment with the moral code they have given for themselves.

For example, I am an Indian. I am a daughter. I am a sister. I am a cousin. I am a friend. I am an employee or a business owner. I am honourable. I am respectful. I am loved. Each of these statements carry a Moral Code for identity, define it and maintain it.

Once you define integrity there are less chances of days being missed and even if you do (just like there is no perfection), the days of missing out will be much less compared to not having a sketch.

INTENTION

This is so important because the world runs on it. For example, even if you want to get up and drink water, your brain sends the message to the body to get up and fill water. Respect yourself and others. We are all humans and get disappointed, it's about just getting present to that and taking an action that can create a WIN-WIN situation for all.

Further, there are some people who can touch something and turn it into gold, like the Midas touch. That is only because they have a habitual practice of doing everything with intention. Just like we spoke about removing any fears and remembering beautiful moments, it's also important to constantly keep in mind the task you're taking up and what you want to accomplish by doing that. This is how sports athletes and others prime themselves before entering the field.

For example, if you're going to date a guy and you know you like him, you can set an intention that this date is meant for the long run and it will generate great results that can lead to marriage, etc.

IMAGINATION

This includes living with a dream as if it already happened, and raising your vibe to that level actually makes it happen. They say imagination is everything. Imagine big things and believe they can happen.

> **"Everything is created twice, once in the mind and then in reality"**
>
> **– Robin S. Sharma**

This is one of the oldest methods used in this field, along with the creative faculty we possess. For example, imagine your office and every detail of it. Everything is a reality because someone imagined it and created it.

If asked to describe your future in three words, what would they be? For me, it would be Love, Matter and Celebrate, meaning, Love (relationships), Matter (to help people get what they want), and Celebrate (enjoy and cherish moments in a state of gratitude). Imagining is also about living your best future positive self now so that over time you become that. Every night before you go to sleep, ask yourself about the three words: did you live them, did you love, did you matter and did you celebrate, and did you live the day fully?

I am sure every person who started from scratch has started here, and today it's not necessary to be a king's son to adorn the throne. You can work towards earning the throne you want to build, or the Empire you want to build.

The majority of their journeys started small; mine did too. It is in our hands to make sure we don't stay there and instead find ways to move ahead. The best way to do this is to be associated with a community which can understand where you are, your journey and tell you that YOU CAN.

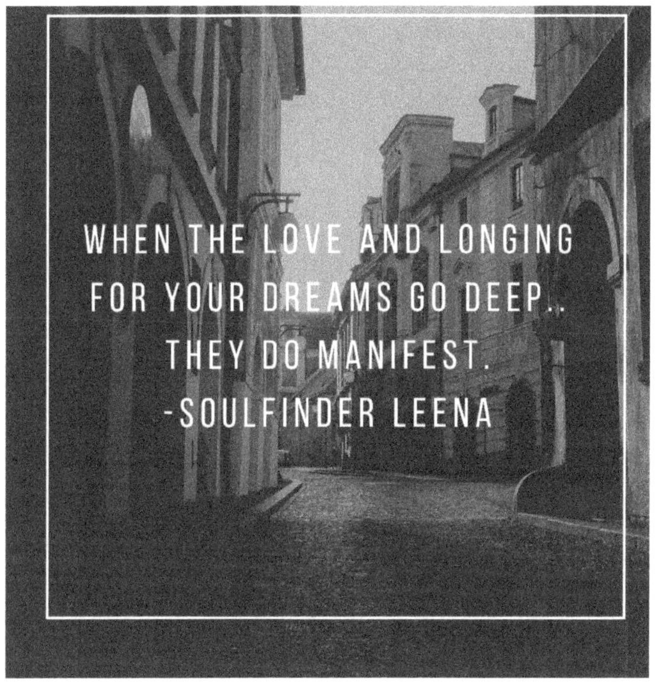
WHEN THE LOVE AND LONGING
FOR YOUR DREAMS GO DEEP...
THEY DO MANIFEST.
-SOULFINDER LEENA

Notes:

2. Believe In A Supreme Power

There are times when things are not in our control and may drive us to feeling stressed or frustrated. However, the Power is truly in trusting that there is something above us all. The being of ours that is guiding us to what we actually need and not simply what we want. This belief also includes trusting that what we get is what is meant to be and that there are reasons behind it.

The biggest example that has taught me this is my dad as he practised Vipassana and then became extremely intuitive. He was so amazing that he could actually sense anything that was about to happen and knew it, like a neem tree falling one day that was right in front of our house. He was so connected to nature. I had the most beautiful days of my life with him in the last six months that he lived. I am deeply thankful to him for leaving me with a spiritual path to follow.

Also, I can say whether or not we agree in our various practices of spirituality, religion, idol worship or having faith in Nature, we are all just trusting the Universe in different ways. Some people have faith in the Unknown, some worship in the form of light, some in the form of sound. Some who don't worship actually do so without realizing it by at least having a belief that they will wake up tomorrow and see a new day, get paid at the end of the month, or work towards their goals, by trusting or having faith in the unknown Source. The Universe has never created different ways or names – it is we humans who have done so. There is a cosmic energy working for sure.

Also, it is important to know that God has created us to be potentially holy. Our task as humans is to find Holiness in what appears to be unholy situations. It is here we learn to nurture our soul. We see beauty in the sunrise, in snow-capped mountains, and the smile of a healthy child. Similarly, we can learn to find the holiness in seemingly unpleasant circumstances too – difficult lessons, a family tragedy or a struggle for life. When we fill our life completely with the desire to see holiness in everyday things, something magical begins to happen. A feeling of peace emerges here. We begin to see nurturing aspects of daily living that were previously hidden to us. Just remember, God's fingerprints are in everything and that alone makes it special.

Some people may question why people are supportive of idol worship. There is both God with Form and without Form. As humans too, we have the physical body and the soul. Ideally by being around the world and listening to others we start living in the physical body. At this stage when we are not practising meditation or haven't learnt to internalise our beliefs, this is where people can just start lighting a candle or a lamp in front of God by stating that I am lighting or awakening all the chakras in my body by lighting /offering the candle. This is the first step for you to start moving towards internalising too, and later you can start practising some meditation.

3. Certainty Is The Enemy Of Growth And High Performance

We all want Certainty in some way or the other amid the chaos in the world. Certainty blinds you or sets false or fixed limits and creates automatic habits that become the not-so-right way of doing or implementing things. A person who is certain is the most closed to learning, and the most vulnerable to dogma. It's about getting over certainty and replacing it with curiosity and genuine self-confidence. We as humans are not made to merely survive, we are made to thrive in a way that we are Creators of our lives. We need to work on bringing that level of transformation to ourselves that can create a beautiful world for us. Some keys to thriving are valuing oneself, adapting to change, feeling the uncertainty and taking action anyway. It is a combination of gratitude, strength and commitment. It is easy to lose the sense of this commitment and courage when experiencing disappointments. We must still continue to move forward. So it is important for us to overcome this habit. Also, to strengthen certainty, especially in uncertain times, it is important for us to be decisive and stick to the decision we made, as the time will come when we will be able to overcome that and make it certain.

Problems, issues and difficulties will come, no matter who you are. We are all subject to our own worries and anxieties, only the flavour is different. We must instead see challenges as opportunities.

Notes:

things started changing
when i changed, things
moved when i moved..
It all began with
me.. I dont live there
anymore.
Leena Chandan

4. Positive Social Interactions

Creating positive interactions is a conscious effort made by people. It is about having thoughts about your future image and how you want to be remembered. We think that someday we'll give time which never happens. Also, it is not about quantity, it is about quality. So make sure you spare some time for your loved ones and peers and make those few minutes for them such that they feel our presence for those few minutes every day. Also, imagine, why would a person after twenty years love me or respect me? It is simply because we added that value each day that builds up for that span of years and earns respect. This journey comes up when you start loving yourself first. My realization to this started when I never took the time to interact much with my mother every day. I noticed there were days when she got disappointed or angry at me for no reason. However, I noticed a huge change in the relationship when I took the initiative of giving 15-20 minutes to her every single day without fail. I started hugging her every single day in addition to giving her 20 minutes. We played Carrom board or Chess. It could be as simple as that. This made us happy and created momentum for our complete day.

5. Developing Hobbies To Pursue Your Passion

Consider taking up hobbies like reading, cooking class, swimming or piano lessons, learning a new language, storytelling, listening skills, or games that make you think. What skills do you want to learn now, and next? A hobby sets you free and gives you more freedom to think and feel the new. It is a meditation by itself to rejuvenate your mood and activate your brain to pursue something that makes you feel good. Further, the art of doing something like this can become a passion to work on as a career in your future if need be. Also, being "Givers to Self" is also a list inclusive in hobbies. The idea is to be consistent in the practice.

Notes:

6. The Key To Attaining The Highest Vibration

I love the way Abraham Hicks says, "Massage your thoughts to feel better and take action." Imagine a telephone provider has a tower from which it sends signals. Similarly, consider there is a Universal Force or Supreme Power that provides us the Energy we need, and it is abundant. It is for us to receive those specifically higher vibrations we need to tune in to that frequency. For example, if we want to listen to 98.3 FM, we have to tune in to the radio and set the frequency to 98.3, then we receive it and we can't listen to the songs on 98.3 on any other setting. Once you realise this, know that that is the way it is in the present moment, then take steps to tune yourself. For example, if we have five major things to achieve on our list and we have received four, what we do is, we go so deep to get the fifth one that we forget to value or care for the wellbeing of the four we have. Conversely, you could have one thing that's received and going well for you and the other four are yet to be received. We can just value and stay tuned into this one thing and then get the other four things we have on the list because "the Receiving Mode is the Receiving Mode." When you believe you have to work hard to make up for inferiority or past wrong doings, or when you feel you have to work really hard to justify your existence, all these things are contrary to what your inner being knows about your readiness and your worthiness. So, you get crosswise with the energy and then you put out more and more effort and then get exhausted. If you're counting your blessings, looking for reasons to feel good in positive aspects, and not having knee-jerk reactions to so many things, then you're in a receiving mode. This Receiving Mode is a Replenishing mode, that's where your vitality, stamina, good ideas, and purpose come from. In return, if we are reacting to what we don't want, we are vibrating in contrast to what we do want.

Let's consider that every Subject is two Subjects:

What is Wanted, and the Absence of It

Sometimes when we think of having money we are also thinking not having enough of it. Sometimes when we are thinking about having or improving a relationship we are also often thinking of the absence of a relationship, or sometimes we have a relationship but it gives us what we don't want. If we don't introduce an understanding to this equation of what our emotions are telling us, then we can't guide our thoughts at early stages, and if we don't guide them in the early stages, then Law of Attraction is going to carry them into greater and greater momentum where you believe that you have to take action, however, there's not enough action to compensate for that momentum that is playing in opposition to what you want. So, what did you understand, and what's the answer to this? It's all about chilling out, being nicer to yourself. Think more thoughts about yourself that feel good, and about others too. Don't work so hard, give yourself a break, get more rest, do things that feel good to you. This is the only way to turn this around. It's true that you can't command yourself into alignment, you cannot put out effort to get yourself into alignment, you have to release, you have to let go. LET GO OF RESISTANCE. Once you let go of the resistance it will flow. Once you stop resisting, your desire comes to be more prominent.

Say to yourself every day before you sleep – I am a Creator of my Reality and I like that. Also, as I sleep tonight, Momentum is going to subside because my thoughts are not going to be active and the Law of Attraction is not going to be reacting to my thoughts. However, the Law of Attraction is going to continue to react to the thoughts of my inner being who never sleeps. By practising this, the potential for your waking up in the morning with the thoughts of your inner being will be dominant. I am going to feel the movement of what my inner being knows, and my beliefs are going to challenge it. Each time that I believe the challenges to the path ahead can be overcome by the thoughts of my inner being, ones of the success and joy that I seek, I will be alleviated from the soft negative emotion. This is what I'll do tomorrow and the following days after that. It won't be 30 days before I would have bridged my beliefs and I'll have the evidence all around me, miracle after miracle, the miracle of breaking through my own resistance. There are only two ways to achieve this: either get the flight going so fast that it won't let the wall of resistance hinder what's hard on you or your flight, or, little by little, release your resistance. This is how creation works and I pray this helps you attain your own reality. Care about the way you feel and choose better-feeling thoughts.

Do you know how you came into being willing to endure negative emotion? Maybe it's because you wanted the contrast to get you to launch your rockets, or maybe you wanted to be hard on yourself to ask in a strong way, or maybe you wanted to deprive yourself of what you really wanted for some time so that you will really care about it. Sometimes, you do that to your kids, wait until your exams get over, or wait until your birthday. Don't we? However, trust me now, when you get it you will love it. So you really train yourself to hold yourself apart from the wellbeing that'll be there all the time.

What would cause you to be willing to deprive yourself of what you want?

Why would you beat yourself up?

It is all again down to self-love to a great extent. The answer is, you don't like yourself very much. The reason you don't like yourself very much is because you're looking to disconnected people to like you, and they don't like you very much. They have their own stories to deal with. It's not that they don't like you because you're not likeable, it's because they are not in a likeable mood. It's not personal. They don't have anything to give you. If you ask them, they'll give you something you don't like. They are deprived of their love and they don't have anything to give you. So, you're going to get used to the same feeling that you've not liked. Your inner being wants to love you but you're not loving yourself. So start by loving yourself and staying connected to your source of wellbeing, and then let love flow through you and to you, and you will receive the most love, and through you, others will, too.

This made a huge shift in the way I think and implement things. It is human to blame either other people or ourselves many times.

Notes:

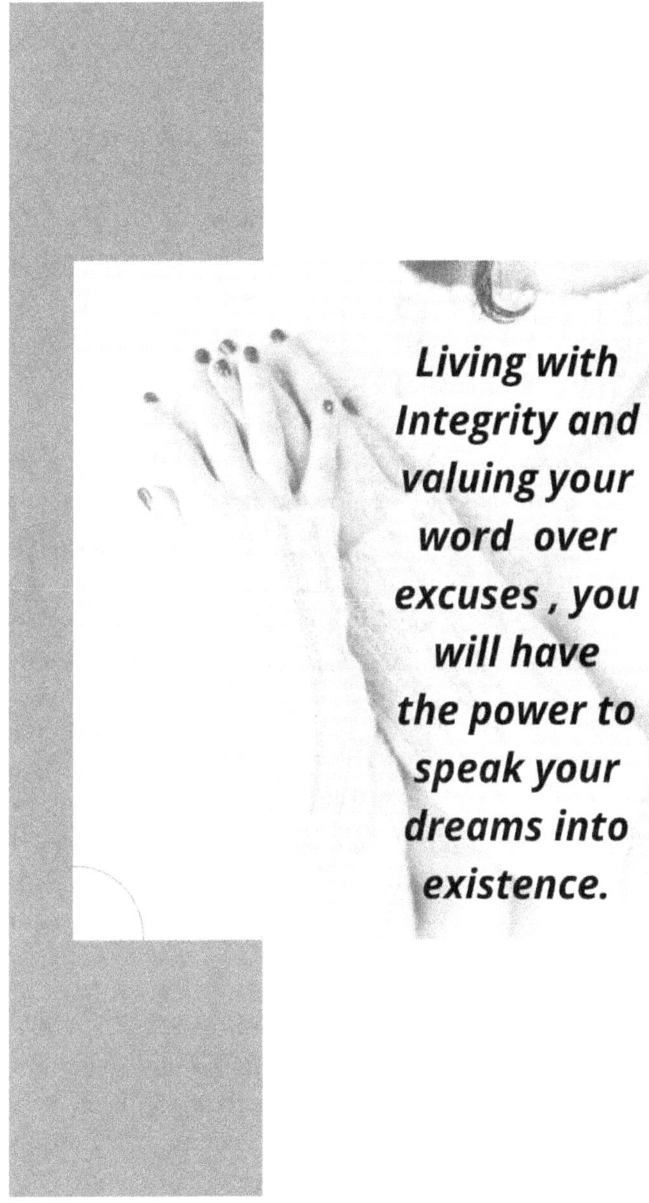
Living with
Integrity and
valuing your
word over
excuses , you
will have
the power to
speak your
dreams into
existence.

7. Procrastination Or Clarity – The Choice Is Yours

In the process of transforming your life from mediocrity to excellence, you have to actually start doing things and taking actions that may or may not be comfortable while cloud of doubts surround your mind. I have a life experience that I can share here. There was a person who worked a 72-hour shift at the fire station, and on his way home stopped at the grocery store. There was a lady who came running to him and hugged in tears, saying, "Thank you!" When he asked what happened, she told him that he was the person who saved her from a fire that happened at her home, and she wanted to share her gratitude. So, you never know how the work you're doing is touching someone's life somewhere and how they give your life purpose. It is very important to keep contributing where we are with dedication, because we will never know whose life we are touching.

Magic happens when you start practising all of the above mentioned tasks of being GIVERS TO SELF on a regular basis and act in spite of feeling lazy, knowing that there is light at the end of the tunnel and huge success waiting for you. The more you become clear, the less you procrastinate.

Seeking clarity is about cultivating a habit of asking questions, looking within, observing your behaviours, and assessing whether you're on track. This will build your momentum, which will increase your productivity, as well as your confidence and desire to do more and be more. And all of this will contribute to your overall happiness.

How can you find clarity? Think about tomorrow, and what do you do to stay connected with what matters today. This will get you engaged and growing. Ask yourself, who are you, and what do you want from life? How do you get it? What are your values, strengths and weaknesses? What do you find meaningful and fulfilling? What are your goals and plans? Clarity is associated with overall self-esteem, which also means that how positively you feel about yourself is associated with how well you know yourself. Clear goals and deadlines create a space of productivity, profitability and satisfaction.

Then ask yourself, what do you need to focus on to stay clear about what matters most? What are you not clear about and how does that affect your performance? What do you do when you feel uncertain? If you were to tell someone the thing that makes you successful, what would it be?

In this context, most of the successful people not only know where they stand today, they also know what skills they'll need to acquire in order to take their next steps into the future to achieve excellence. They focussed not only on themselves, but also on how they could help others get what they wanted.

If you are someone lacking clarity, it's absolutely fine because you can learn to develop it. But clarity cannot be merely hoped for from a flash of inspiration. The best way to acquire it is to keep asking yourself relevant questions about what you want next, trying new things, and doing constant research.

A high-performing waiter would be obsessed over his service towards his customer not only because it is his job, but also because he cares about his customer's experience and the restaurant's future reputation. It's about creating fans to serve a larger vision.

It is when someone gets disconnected from the future and their contribution to it that they underperform. The simple reason being they don't find tomorrow exciting, so they stop performing today.

This was nothing like me, initially. I would say I have been the laziest person you could have known. It's good to be lazy, but don't stop looking for a path. I have also worked endlessly at times when I had direction. So now you know that you'll stop being in the zone of procrastination if you're clear about what to do, and hence you can start defining it now.

Go ☺.......... Go ☺.......... Go ☺............... if you don't know the path yet, just get up, dress up and show up where you are, anyway. You will still find a way. ☺

Also, what do you want?

What in your life will give you the greatest meaning?

What kind of person do you want to be while you are doing this?

How should you treat others?

What are the intentions and objectives that define you?

What can you focus on that will bring you a sense of connection and fulfilment?

Further, with clarity it is very important to eliminate things that don't matter. See how you could position yourself and your relationships in a different way in your industry while also identifying what is beyond the expected so that it turns out excellent.

Another thing to consider is feelings. When we are about to perform, there can be fear or other emotions that pop up. However, high performers show emotional intelligence and choose to flow with a better feeling by having control over their emotions. They remind themselves of some happy moment as they prepare to perform. There also has to be a conscious effort to be in the present, and show confidence, flow and joy. ☺

Notes:

8. Thinking Positive Vs. Being Positive

Thinking positive means I know in my mind that I have sown a seed of positivity, and hence the result will be positive. However, being positive means that, even if my present is cloudy and not in that golden moment of success, I can still feel it, visualise it and behave like I have already achieved it. This contributes in a big way to shift your vibration to attract all that you want.

I came across a client whom I was helping with transformation. In the process of identifying his mind blocks, he was not willing to believe that he could find a person as a companion at the age of 50. Do you agree with me that it is so common nowadays that people do get married in their 50s or at least some in their 40s? When I work with him and he doesn't open his mind to deeply program a new perspective that yes, it is possible that he can find someone, will I be able to successfully coach him? Similarly, when you get an idea, cultivate the habit of viewing things with a different perspective, and why the person is saying what they are. What is it that he can do to take action and truly make it happen? First, he would need to accept his situation as is. Then he needs to believe that it is possible for him to find a partner that he wants, and is willing do whatever it takes to make this happen, which is the action mode.

What helps me lift up my energy and vibration to a level where success is possible?

The Situation cycle: The act of telling yourself you're going to have a great day, amazing day, blissful day not only helps convince you mentally, it sets off chemical triggers in your brain which affect your mental state. You may have noticed that when you start with a tough day for some reason, the whole day becomes tough. It's a chain reaction. So, be sure to start your day with silence and those practices that can make your day amazing.

9. Always Start Any Task By Keeping The End In Mind

> ***With all Clarity,***
> ***No absurdity,***
> ***Through Adversity,***
> ***For Eternity.***
> ***To Infinity.***
> ***Absolutely***
>
> ***– Reeca Dae Rettig.***

A ship that is sailing without knowing its destination will stay in the middle of the sea going nowhere. So practice things that give you clarity in your direction and you will know where you're headed. This seemed the most difficult thing for me to achieve because I believed that we should accept life as it comes and just live it the way it is, not expecting much, and what was I left with? Failure everywhere. I am glad that following the GIVERS practice got me here and I am very clear about everything I want from my life now. I have practised it for over three years to get here, and the day I started running towards my dreams, I felt unstoppable. I literally got to a place where I spent all my money in coaching myself and more. I would do anything I could to gain clarity. When the destination is known, so much can be created, and new opportunities will open up.

10. High Performers See And Serve Above And Beyond Their Strengths

It is good for us to understand and be aware of our innate strengths and goals. High performers have high levels of energy, never get distracted, know what to focus on, and have high levels of courage. They are bold, speaking up for themselves and their ideas. They take action, take risks, and are extremely productive. However, to be a high performer we have to be open to seeing beyond what comes naturally to us and see instead how we can best lead. It's more about adapting yourself to a service. High performers do not only look at what they are good at. They look to see what is required to be of service to deliver that, grow from it and lead others to it as well. They focus on what gives them an edge so they can have an impact.

They also are admired for a specific ability to contribute- a specific benefit such as deep knowledge, a highly priced skill or an elite network. They aim to be absolutely exceptional in one area in spite of having a reputation for being good at most things. In this situation, it is very important to understand your own value, or else we cannot expect others to understand us.

11. Being At Peace With Imperfection

Perfection is a good practice in order to be organised, but it's not good to overdo it. The need for perfection and inner tranquillity conflict with each other. The attachment to having something in a particular way better than it is already is losing the battle. There is a thin line between creating something you are content with and grateful for, and expecting perfection from something by focussing on what's wrong with it and the need to fix it. Focussing on what's wrong clearly implies we are dissatisfied and discontent.

Whether we are focussing on our own shortcomings- a disorganised closet due lack of time, a scratch on the car, an imperfect accomplishment, a few pounds we would like to lose, or someone else's– the way someone looks, behaves or lives their life -- this very act of focussing on imperfection takes us away from our goal of being kind and accepting. Doing so stops you from doing your best by being overly attached to and focused on what's wrong with life. It simply means that there is always a better way to do something. You can enjoy and appreciate the way things already are in this moment.

It takes conscious effort to catch yourself when you fall into a habit of insisting that things should be in a particular way. Gently remind yourself that life is okay the way it is. In the absence of judgement, everything will be fine. As you begin to eliminate your need for perfection in all areas of your life, you will begin to discover the perfection in life itself.

Notes:

12. Get Comfortable With Being Uncomfortable

It's about having conversations with those that you were not comfortable with. It's about doing things you have never done. For example, I was a pampered child and always had a hot water shower. One way of getting uncomfortable for me was to start taking a cold water shower for 21 days. Also, working towards my goal endlessly and connecting with people on a deeper level became a part of my work. I focused on valuing myself, valuing everything I do, and valuing my money and my relationships more. It is common to not open up about your discomfort with other people, however, I connected with an individual and opened up pages of myself that I was not comfortable sharing with others. The views he shared with me actually gave me new insights and a new way to think and act going forward. I resolved my life and learned how to help others resolve their lives for the better.

I know a lady in my office and she was determined to go for an international trip. She did not go out with her friends on weekends and didn't spend any money – she actually saved her lakhs and went with her parents within the year. So you can make anything happen if you're determined to do so.

It's not easy. Ease is not the point. Growth is the point here. There's a lot of work here to go above and beyond everything that does not come easily for you.

As a Coach too, we have to put tough questions to clients sometimes to push them to think out of their comfort zone to challenge them and demand that they give their all. Now that you chose this book, I am sure you're ready for the journey.

If Howard Schultz had given up after being turned down by banks and investors 217 times, there would be no STARBUCKS.

So Buckle up and say NO EXCUSES!

13. The Power Of Repetition

> *"We are what we repeatedly do. Excellence then is not an act but a habit."*
>
> *- Will Durant*

I know how to be happy, healthy and wealthy. Always have a mentor, a coach and do exactly what they tell you, because when I did that, I got everything I wanted. Growth is a part of life. What's not growing is dying. We cannot stay where we are and get better results. When I started, I owed a lot of money to people. Ask yourself, why are you where you are today? Why are people where they are? The obvious answer is, people should have goals. There is energy in the other layers of our body as well the outer layers of the body which they call aura and more. There are specific cameras available to see through the energy field. We as humans are conscious about our physical self – if we are at a beach in Goa we know we are there physically. But mentally, where do we reside and why are we stuck? This energy is a part of the mental program that has almost exclusive control over habitual behaviour, and almost all of our behaviour is habitual. So, it's these energies that are controlling our lives. It really does not matter how hard you work or how many hours of work you put in – until the energy changes, the results will pretty much be the same from one year to the next. When these energies stay in control, nothing changes. So, how do we control this flow of energy to be stable? This can be controlled by keeping certain practices:

A) Constant repetition of the same ideas and/or habits that are opposite to the undesired energy state.

   This repetition can include meditation, exercises, affirmations and more.

B) The second option is experiencing a very rare occurrence that creates a huge emotional impact, like the novel Corona virus that changed the world perspective in many ways.

14. Constant Refining

Once you build a habit and tune your subconscious mind, it is also important to elevate your habit to become your next best self and stay relevant. The world gets more complex as you seek greater success. It is good to have consistency in programming or the methods being practiced. However, its not be done blindly. It requires self-awareness and being alive and present in that moment while practising, and that should also let you probe and check what else you can add on to it. What can you do to automate it? Those at the top never stop learning, they never stop smart practice. It's better to have a mentor who is ahead of you to guide you and your pathway and help you discuss and update you with new ways to keep advancing your practice.

For example, this book has several quotes and conversations in several topics. Pick a topic and see if something new and creative that comes to your mind about this concept. How you can implement this in your life?

The most prevalent complaint most people have is they are not good with technology. Apparently, it's a necessity and there's nothing we can do about it. We have to overcome the fear and learn step by step and practise it in a way that helps. Similarly, the tech guys would be aiming at doing constant research on new gadgets, etc. and updating the world which creates an edge.

Also, at times you will have to get ready to invite new things or take on a new path and that's when it gets most difficult. It really takes deep faith to wait with patience and it takes a lot to trust the path. It's important to do it even then.

Notes:

15. We've All Heard It – Are We Really Practising It?

> *"To forgive is the highest, most beautiful form of love. In return you will receive untold peace and Happiness."*
>
> *– Robert Muller.*

This practice of forgiving something or someone every single day is a most beautiful thing, the letting go of the hostility and hatred that you may have bottled up. When you hold a grudge against someone, it is almost as if you carry that person around on your back with you. It drains your energy and vibration. Forgiveness is an act of spirit and personal courage. By forgiving, you're telling yourself that you are willing to let go of the past and look forward to a new creation. It also shows that you value the relationship more than your ego.

One important thing to keep in mind at this phase is we are not perfect ourselves, so then how can we expect that from someone else?

I would like to share a story from one of my clients here. He was not willing to forgive his mother for some reason. He shared that they'd done a lot of ego clashing and he was not in a state to resolve it. When we spoke he had a lot of anger and frustration toward her. This is something that we carry in relationships and we end up making them bitter over the long term without realising that carrying this bitterness can actually affect us in unknown places.

Just imagine if the person is dead in front of you- would you fight with him/her? How long do we have to carry such things? It's a simple thing to apologize and move on. Forgiveness is the foundation of any meaningful, deep relationship. To just let go and say sorry when we have hurt somebody is what makes the relationship profound. It clearly shows you value the relationship more than being right. It is a choice between being right and being love. Choose love. ☺

16. Charity - - Discover the Joy of Giving

> **"The smallest act of kindness is worth more than the greatest Intention."**
>
> **– Oscar Wilde**

Although we have heard this in every religion, I never believed this to be true until I heard this a few years ago in a motivational talk that it is so important to set aside at least 10 % or 5% of your salary for charity, and I immediately began practising this. It is like sowing a seed and giving it water, sunlight and all the basic needs so the plant will find a way to grow. This is one of the oldest suggestions that anyone can offer, and it is spoken of very well in every religion in its own way. This is a call for those who are not yet doing it. It is like a glorious embellishment that you can add to the beauty of your life. The reason I would call it this is because there will be Givers and the one who is capable of giving is blessed. It needs takers also on the other side to accept gracefully, without which the Circle of Life would be incomplete.

17. Save

> **"Don't save what is left after spending, but spend what is left after saving."**
>
> **- Warren Buffet.**

It is true being a part of the millennial generation we are just not used to saving.

I was so deeply connected to this quote and it entirely changed my life.

This is something I took a very long time to learn. When I had a job, I lavishly spent all my money on shopping, although it was due to frustrating situations, I lived with and it's not an excuse. The most beautiful thing is to accept the situation as it is and let it create a better future for you. Once I practised this, the way I looked at things changed completely. It is extremely important to first pay yourself by saving at least 10% minimum - more is better. People gradually increase their savings to 15, 20 or even 30% to assure financial freedom.

18. Being Responsive, Not Reactive

> *"Reactive people are driven by feelings, by circumstances, by conditions, by their environment. Proactive people are driven by values -- carefully thought about, selected and internalised values."*
>
> *– Stephen Covey.*

Once you become present to the moment you're living in by practicing mindfulness, you realise this is so important because everything we react to has a repercussion. We need to constantly remain conscious to this so that we do not contribute to creating repercussions. Also keep in mind that we're human, so if we do create it, prepare to face it and be human enough to accept it by making great effort to bring the transformation that is required. You can start working on being responsive by first learning that any attack we experience is never personal. It could be due the other person's inner state. If you know yourself well enough, you surely know your self-worth, so they will not be able to affect you as much. For example, if your significant other, parent or teacher annoys you, you can stop in the moment to manage your emotions and then respond later. Another example, if someone stamps your shoes, that's the most annoying thing that could happen, so just relax and either think that they were in a hurry, or missed seeing it rather than simply reacting. One more example comes from the game of cricket. The players use a tactic sledging where the opposing team tries to shout in an abusive way to distract the players of the other team to make the team lose focus. These players have to intently practice patience so they will not take it personally or allow it to affect their focus or the game. Sachin Tendulkar is a good example of maintaining this kind of patience.

Notes:

19. An Era Of Collaborating, Selling And Business Creation

It is absolutely fine to work and collaborate as an employee and earn a living doing so as long as it makes you happy. There is nothing wrong with that. The challenge I faced was that I felt like a misfit working where I did, and that's why I struggled so much in searching for what I wanted until I finally found my purpose. I know so many of my friends who are very happy serving people as managers or team leaders, or serving customers directly. They love what they do and I am happy for them.

My Dear Patrons, on another side, if you're uncomfortable or unused to change, please learn to adapt to bigger changes in life. It is a huge mind shift from being an employee to owning a business for those who do not want to work for someone else. We have to start looking for what we love to do as a passion. So start asking yourself questions and internalising what exactly you would like to become. What is that which you would love doing at any time of the day? This shift also refers to digital products and a gig economy, which means not being paid monthly. You will get paid for your services per hour, such as providing mental health, home-grown food, gaming, healthcare, digital services, affiliate marketing and more.

20. The Company You Keep Matters.

"The better you are at surrounding yourself with people of high potential, the greater your chance for success."

– John.C Maxwell.

Build your family outside of family. Be part of a community outside of your community. This is important as genuine people will keep you accountable for a task (especially a community of coaching) so even if you fall back at times, they won't let you stay there. In my search for clarity, I have become associated with some amazing communities, and I am also in the process of creating my own community.

This will be a community that will co-ordinate knowledge and effort in a spirit of harmony, between two or more people to achieve a purpose. The initial stage of building this cooperative relationship will be to improve your relationship with yourself first. Once that is taken care of, you will be permitted to work with others. There is only a certain level of growth that can be achieved by working independently. Our growth can multiply when we learn to work in co-ordination with others. So, it is very important to have a successful collaboration.

"You will get what you want in life if you help enough other people get what they want."

- Zig Ziglar

21. Success Is The Progressive Realisation Of A Worthy Ideal

As Earl Nightingale puts it in his video, The Strangest Secret, "success is actually a journey to be enjoyed and relished, and the bars of success need to be raised to have an ongoing process of growth." You cannot remain sitting as though in a cocoon in a corner in order to get there. It is not even an end to wait for. So, keep working towards your next goal and celebrate when you achieve it. Then raise your bar for the next goal.

Why is it that someone who might work in a simple profession like teaching be happy, while someone else who is working in a beautiful place earning a huge amount of money is sad? It's simply because the teacher is happy being a teacher, but that employee in the beautiful place deep inside wants to be something else and is just working. It's not wrong to be working to fulfil your responsibilities, but be very sure that you are where you want to be and are happy doing what you're doing. If not, ask yourself what you want to instead become, and find a way to make it happen. The day you are pursuing what you want in life, you are successful!

I love this quote by Jack Canfield – **"I choose to believe things are possible, even when I don't know how they will happen."**

He also talks about a 100%- No- Exception rule. Come what may, you should not compromise on daily disciplines. They have to be a non-negotiable practice. It's a closed door and you have to do it. There is no possibility and hence you do not have to deal with that indecisiveness every day. It makes life easier and helps you focus. It frees up a lot of energy that you would otherwise spend continuing to battle indecision.

To begin, make a list of those things that you want to remove from your everyday activity, keeping only those which will help you develop and be productive, to which you will commit to taking constant action. It is helpful to be in a community where you will be accountable for this. Then you can create an arrangement with an accountability partner in which you will mutually agree to give something in return for every time you miss one of your daily disciplines.

Checklist:

The emotions I have been experiencing a lot lately are....

The areas of life where I am not having the feelings I want are...

The feelings I want to experience in my life include....

The next time I have a negative emotion come up, the thing I am going to say to myself is....

There are two elements to this: Logic and Magic. Both happen – you have to find a way to strike a balance, and that is the art to achieving a fulfilled life.

Also, we need to make a conscious effort to stop seeing a problem as a problem. We need to start looking it at as an adventure. It is as important to enjoy the adventure as it is to get results. This makes the problem smaller. While it doesn't mean that problems stop, it does mean that you can become strong enough to face them with courage.

22. Having Goals And A Vision Board For You

Goal setting is a traditional standard many of us have followed. If combined with the practice of being "Givers to Self" and setting Smart goals which are Specific, Measurable, Attainable, Relevant and Time-based, the complete view of thinking about goals changes every day. We'll keep looking every day at what we can do to enhance or add on to our goals list. Another way to approach your goals list is to create a vision board for them. Write down and post on it the dates of what you want to achieve, by when, why you want it, and how you will take action toward achieving it.

There was once a Hollywood movie actor who was out of work for years and had nothing. When he heard about this vision board idea, he just wrote a note and placed it next to his bed stating that he would have 60,000 dollars by the end of the year. He read it every single day and visualised many directors approaching him and giving him wonderful opportunities and paying him a lot of money. Then he took action to get it. It worked! He actually received a check in exactly that same amount before the date came due. So start imagining and creating visuals of what exactly you want, and stay associated with the right people who can support you, encourage you, and keep you accountable to achieving your dreams, and attaining them will be possible.

I would suggest you keep this book someplace within your sight so you can open any page to read a topic, constantly create what you want, stay committed to doing so, and continue to take action. I am sure you will achieve your goals.

Write a description of your future self about how you could be better than you are today. Then start bringing that state to the present by working towards it to become that person and fulfilling those dreams.

Checklist:

- Three things in which I would like to become extraordinary right now are ...
- My why's for becoming excellent in each of these areas...
- I will affirm myself with and say it out loud to myself - I am ...
- Biggest goal I want to achieve...
- My five moves to achieve my goal swiftly are ....
- Five people who have achieved that dream whom I could study..
- The less-important activities I'll cut from my schedule are..
- What was the greatest lesson each person taught you about life?
- What values or traits are you inspired to embody in your own life?

Notes:

There is no Self-Made Man

> *"Lives are changed when people connect. Life is changed when everything is connected.*
>
> *– Qualcomm motto.*

All in all, concluding my thoughts in the words of Brendon Burchard:

"Seek clarity, generate energy, raise necessity, increase productivity, develop influence and demonstrate courage."

Learning and implementing all the above-mentioned practices doesn't mean you will become a super human, or that you need to. You have flaws; we all do. The only thing you'll tell yourself is, "Now I finally know what it takes to be my best. I am confident in my abilities to figure out a way to succeed for the rest of my life."

In the process of writing this book, I became present to so much more than I previously had in terms of Relationships with everything around, every individual, and Myself. I am positive you enjoyed reading my book and it's an energizer to walk your way to Success.

Write to me @ soulfinder0003@gmail.com – feel free to share what you loved most about the book.

One-to-One Coaching services specifically for those who want to create an impactful transformation in their life. (for relationships and more)

Join us on the Face book page The Relationship Code for Everything by Leena Chandan for more activities, advances and knowledge-sharing.

I acknowledge and thank all those people who supported me in publishing this book and I am happy to express my deep gratitude for You, Dear Reader, for allowing me to be a part of your life.

My next book will be launched soon and it is called The Relationship Code for Love.

It is my prayer and wish that you and your family live in Bliss forever☺

Happiness is not only a
choice. its a Responsibility.
Soulfinder Leena Chandan

www.ingramcontent.com/pod-product-compliance
Lightning Source LLC
La Vergne TN
LVHW051149200726
843495LV00025B/1816